STANLEY GOBBLE WHOPPER

Helps a Pumpkin Grow

Peperz Pumpkin Patch is a magical pumpkin patch where every day new pumpkins are born. Most folks don't know this, but it is six blocks long, which of course makes it the longest pumpkin patch in the entire galaxy!! At night, an explosion of orange burst in the sky, and rumor has it that this is when the pumpkins come alive, just like humans, with feet, hands, and faces.

Shoo

Clouds

Shoo

The watcher of the pumpkin patch is a gnome named Stanley, who has a giant cone hat, giant feet, and two itty bitty black eyes. His job is to keep away the dirt bugs and make sure that the pumpkins always have enough water and sun.

Come Clouds Come

When there is too much rain, he calls up to the clouds, "shoo Clouds shoo"! When there is too much sun, he calls out "come clouds come"! Without Stanley, the dirt bugs would take over the pumpkin patch or the pump-kins would have too much rain or sun. The pumpkins love Stanley for all he does.

One day after all the kids have gone home, Stanley hears light crying and sniffles coming from the middle of the patch. He doesn't see anything but soon spots a tiny pumpkin. Stanley goes over and asks, "What's your name, little one?" The tiny pumpkin sniffles, then replies, "Sprelley." "Well, what's wrong?" asked Stanley. The tiny pumpkin explains that other pumpkins tease her, and it makes her sad. So Stanley invited her to come and have a cup of juice at his house.

Little Sprelley started drinking the juice from a swirly whirly curly straw

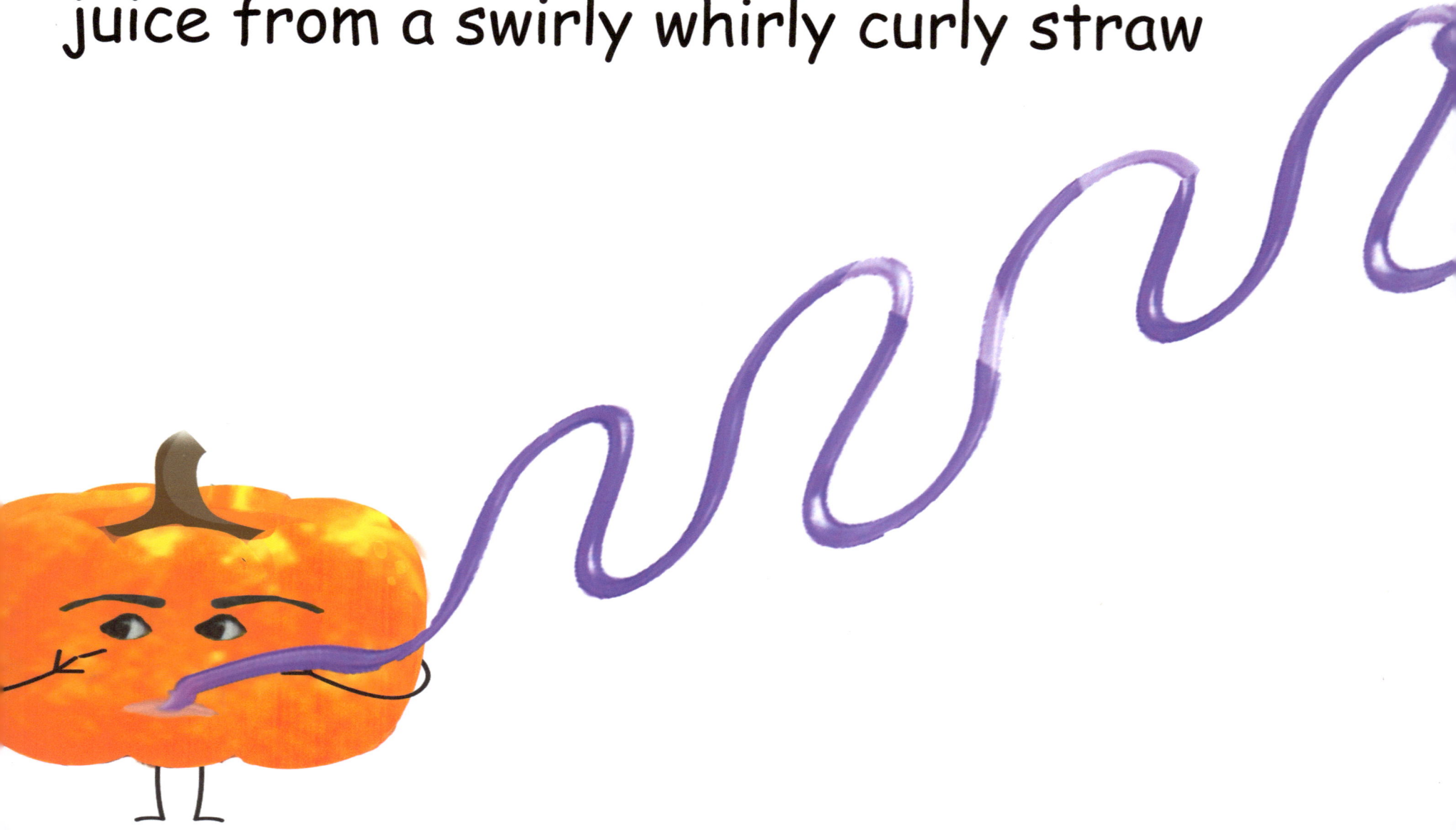

and shared with Stanley how sad she has felt lately because she had no friends to play with.

"This morning, I saw Buster playing with his dinosaurs. He was wearing a really cool dinosaur hat. So, I went up to him and said, "Can I play with you?" Buster just laughed at me and said, "NO, YOU ARE TOO SMALL!"

Tiny sweet Sprelley continued, "So then I thought I might go play with Queen Amorah, she always looks so pretty in her spicy red jewels and crown. I thought maybe she would play dress-up with me, but she didn't. She had only ugly words to say to me that made me sad. "No, tiny pumpkins are not allowed in my kingdom." So I cried myself to sleep that night.

Stanley tells Sprelley about a magical potion he has that will make her grow. Together they followed a bright light, and then Stanley opened a cabinet using a giant key.

Stanley gives Sprelley the potion and tells her, "As you take a sip every day, you will grow bigger and bigger, and soon you will be the biggest pumpkin in Peperz Patch." With hesitation, Sprelley takes the first sip, and her eyes shine bright just like the magical potion bottle. "Yummy! This is sweet and sour, just the way I like it," said Sprelley.

Weeks went by, and Stanley watched as Sprelley grew bigger and stronger.

The tiny, sad, pumpkin now has many friends and has indeed grown to be the biggest pumpkin around.

One day, Sprelley asked Stanley for more juice since the potion bottle was empty, Sprelley had drunk every drop.

The only magic was you!

Stanley simply replied, "As for the potion, I have no more. But it wasn't the potion that made you grow, water and patience are the ingredients of the magical potion. Fear no more for the only magic was you.

Patience

Contributing Authors

CALEB FASSLER

ELIANA SOTELO

Caleb Fassler: is ten years old and wants to be a firefighter when he grows up. He would like to be a YouTuber for a side job and currently has his own YouTube channel where he makes gameplay videos and cartoons. He loves video games and riding his electric scooter. Caleb is fun-loving and a very genuine person and very artistic.

Eliana Sotelo: is six years old and wants to be the President when she grows up. She loves to do gymnastics and play with her LOL dolls. Eliana is fun, outgoing, and caring. She loves her family and friends.

DARIAN J. RENDEN

JSERIE "SKAII" SHIELDS

Darian J. Renden: is seven years old and wants to be a Paleontologist when he grows up. He loves to read all about Dinosaurs. He also likes to play soccer and Pokémon Go. Darian is an energetic child who loves to learn and do things.

JJserie "Skaii" Shields: is eleven years old. The youngest of 5. She wants to be a police officer when she gets older. Her passion is modeling and acting. She is also signed with a modeling agency. She loves to dance, draw, and run track. She is a very loving person and loves everybody. She's a great leader and always sets a great example.

Your Children Our

Stories

CSB
INNOVATIONS

www.csbinnovations.com

www.ingramcontent.com/pod-product-compliance
Lightning Source LLC
Chambersburg PA
CBHW040406100426

42811CB00017B/1851